# A Note to Parents

DK READERS is a compelling program for beginning readers, designed in conjunction with leading literacy experts, including Dr. Linda Gambrell, Director of the School of Education at Clemson University. Dr. Gambrell has served on the Board of Directors of the International Reading Association and as President of the National Reading Conference.

Beautiful illustrations and superb full-color photographs combine with engaging, easy-to-read stories to offer a fresh approach to each subject in the series. Each DK READER is guaranteed to capture a child's interest while developing his or her reading skills, general knowledge, and love of reading.

The five levels of DK READERS are aimed at different reading abilities, enabling you to choose the books that are exactly right for your child:

**Pre-level 1:** Learning to read
**Level 1:** Beginning to read
**Level 2:** Beginning to read alone
**Level 3:** Reading alone
**Level 4:** Proficient readers

The "normal" age at which a child begins to read can be anywhere from three to eight years old, so these levels are intended only as a general guideline.

No matter which level you select, you can be sure that you are helping your child learn to read, then read to learn!

LONDON, NEW YORK, MUNICH,
MELBOURNE, and DELHI

**Editor** Dawn Sirett
**Art Editor** Jane Horne
**Senior Editor** Linda Esposito
**Senior Art Editor** Diane Thistlethwaite
**US Editor** Regina Kahney
**Production** Melanie Dowland
**Picture Researcher** Cynthia Frazer
**Jacket Designer** Karen Lieberman
**Natural History Consultant**
Theresa Greenaway
**Reading Consultant**
Linda B. Gambrell, Ph.D.

First American Edition, 2000
06 07 08 09 20 19 18 17 16 15 14 13 12 11
Published in the United States by DK Publishing, Inc.
375 Hudson Street, New York, New York 10014

Published in Great Britain by Dorling Kindersley Limited

Library of Congress Cataloging-in-Publication Data
Wallace, Karen.
A bed for the winter / by Karen Wallace -- 1st American ed.
p. cm. -- (Dorling Kindersley readers)
Summary: a dormouse encounters many different animals as she
searches for a place to spend the winter.
ISBN-13: 978-0-7894-5706-6 ISBN-10: 0-7894-5706-7(hc)
ISBN-13: 978-0-7894-5707-3 ISBN-10: 0-7894-5707-5(pb)
1. Hibernation--Juvenile literature. 2. Hazel mouse--Hibernation--Juvenile
literature. [1. Dormice. 2. Animals--Habitations. 3. Hibernation.]
I. Title. II. Series.

QL755.W36 2000
591.56'5--dc21                                    99-049697

Color reproduction by Colourscan, Singapore
Printed and bound in China by L Rex Printing Co., Ltd

The publisher would like to thank the following for
their kind permission to reproduce their photographs:
Key: a=above, c=center, b=below, l=left, r=right, t=top
**Heather Angel**: 11 tr, 13 tr, 15 br; **Ardea London Ltd**: Ian Beames 1 br, 9 br,
17 inset, 17 br, 19 tr, 32 cra, R. J. C. Blewitt 23 t, Rosie Bomford 6–7 t, M.
Watson 4–5 b, 21 br; **Bruce Coleman Collection Ltd**: Antonio Manzanares
14 inset, 32 tr, William S. Paton 16–17 b, 20–21 b, Hans Reinhard 3 b, 25 br,
Jens Rydell 14–15 t, Kim Taylor 7 b, 30–31, Colin Varndell 24–25 t;
**Ecoscene**: R. Redfern 29 t; **NHPA**: John Shaw 12–13 b; **Oxford Scientific
Films**: G. I. Bernard 17 t, Scott Camazine 30 tl, tr, cra, br, Philippe Henry 12
cl, 32 bl, Michael Leach 28 b, T. C. Nature 10–11 b, K. G. Vock/Okapia 22 b;
**Papilio Photographic**: 8–9 t; **Planet Earth Pictures**: Richard Coomber 22 cra,
32 crb; **Science Photo Library**: cover (snowflakes); **Telegraph Colour
Library**: 5 c, 32 tl, Steve Bloom 26 t, Philip Chapman 26–27 b; **Tony Stone
Images**: cover (trees)

Additional photography for DK:
Geoff Brightling, Peter Chadwick, Mike Dunning,
Frank Greenaway, Dave King, and Kim Taylor.
All other images © Dorling Kindersley.
For further information see: www.dkimages.com

Discover more at

# www.dk.com

DK READERS

BEGINNING TO READ 1

# A Bed for the Winter

Written by Karen Wallace

DK Publishing, Inc.

A fluffy-tailed dormouse
stops by a meadow.

Cold rain is falling.
Soon snow will be coming.

The dormouse is looking
for somewhere to sleep.
She needs a bed for the winter.

meadow

A squirrel gathers leaves
high in a tree.
He makes his nest warm
for the cold winter weather.

nest

But a nest in the treetops
is too high for a dormouse.
The dormouse looks up,
then scurries by.

A queen wasp sleeps
under an oak stump.
She has squeezed through
a crack in the rotten wood.

stump

But a crack in an oak stump
is too small for a dormouse.
The dormouse looks in,
then scurries by.

9

A golden-eyed toad sleeps
under a stone.
It is muddy and wet
and the toad's skin is cold.

But it's too wet for a dormouse
under a stone.
The dormouse looks in,
then scurries by.

A mother brown bear
sleeps in a den.
She is furry and warm.
She stretches and yawns.

den

The dormouse looks in.
The bear's teeth are huge!
The dormouse trembles …
then scurries by.

cave

Bats hang in a cave
and cling to the rock.
They huddle together
and sleep through the winter.

The cave is damp and dark.
It's too cold for a dormouse.
The dormouse looks in,
then scurries by.

A family of rabbits
hop into their burrow.
They live underground
when the weather is cold.
But there are too many rabbits
to make room for a dormouse.

burrow

The dormouse
looks in,
then scurries by.

17

An owl
with sharp claws
flies over the meadow.
He is hungry
and watchful.
He is hunting
for mice.

The owl swoops!
The dormouse
hides in a bush.

Where can she find
a safe bed
for the winter?

A deer comes to the meadow.
She nibbles the grass.
Her coat has grown thick
for the cold winter weather.

The dormouse shivers in the wind,
then scurries by.

A storm is coming.
The sky has turned black.

Bees fly home
to their hive.

hive

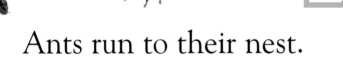

Ants run to their nest.

The dormouse waits
under a branch
for the storm to pass by.
Where can she find
a safe bed for the winter?

A snake slides through the grass.

He has hungry black eyes.

He stares at the dormouse.

His tongue flicks in and out.

The dormouse
is trapped.
She's too scared
to move.

The snake slithers closer.
His forked tongue comes nearer.

BOOM!
Thunder rumbles.
CRACK!
Lightning flashes.

The snake stops for a second,
then shoots into the grass.

The dormouse runs
through the meadow.
Her heart pounds like a drum.
She climbs up a tree trunk.

tree trunk

She crawls into a hole.
She finds a place
that is safe and dry!

Snow falls on the meadow.
The ground is
frozen and hard.
Snug in the tree hole,
the dormouse is sleeping.
Her long, fluffy tail
is wrapped tightly
around her.

Her search is over.
The dormouse is safe.
At last she has found
her bed for the winter!

# Picture Word List

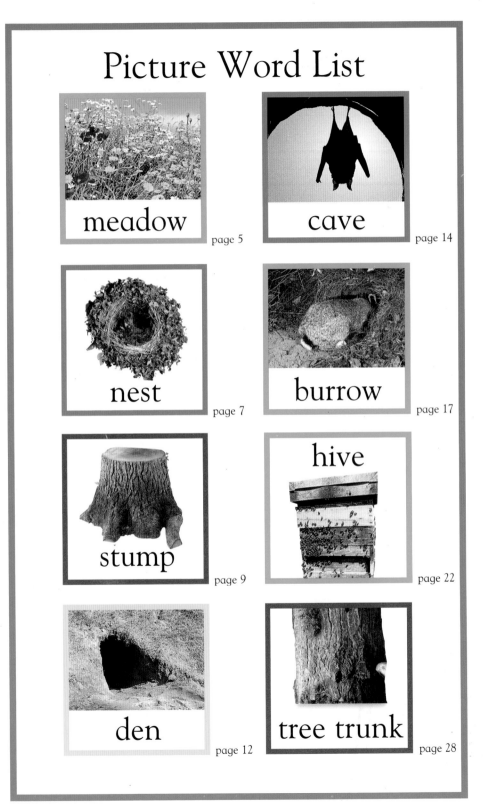

meadow
page 5

cave
page 14

nest
page 7

burrow
page 17

stump
page 9

hive
page 22

den
page 12

tree trunk
page 28